PRESIDENTS OF THE U.S.A.

FRANKLIN PIERCE

OUR FOURTEENTH PRESIDENT

by Steven Ferry

THE CHILD'S WORLD ®

The Child's World®

Published in the United States of America

The Child's World®
1980 Lookout Drive • Mankato, MN 56003-1705
800-599-READ • www.childsworld.com

Acknowledgments
The Child's World®: Mary Berendes, Publishing Director

Creative Spark: Mary McGavic, Project Director; Melissa McDaniel, Editorial Director; Deborah Goodsite, Photo Research

The Design Lab: Kathleen Petelinsek, Design; Gregory Lindholm, Page Production

Content Adviser: David R. Smith, Adjunct Assistant Professor of History, University of Michigan–Ann Arbor

Photos
Cover and page 3: White House Historical Association (White House Collection)(detail); White House Historical Association (White House Collection)

Interior: The Art Archive: 14, 22, 34 (Culver Pictures); Art Resource, NY: 15, 32 (National Portrait Gallery, Smithsonian Institution), 30 (The Metropolitan Museum of Art); Associated Press Images: 20 and 38; Bowdoin College Museum of Art, Brunswick, Maine: 7; The Bridgeman Art Library: 8 (Peabody Essex Museum, Salem, Massachusetts, USA), 9 (Chicago History Museum, USA), 19 (Collection of the New-York Historical Society, USA); Corbis: 33 (Bettmann), 36 (Lee Snider/Photo Images); The Granger Collection, New York: 4, 10, 16 and 38, 23, 24, 26, 27, 28, 29, 31 and 39, 35; The Image Works: 5 (Andre Jenny); iStockphoto: 44 (Tim Fan); Library of Congress: 18; New Hampshire Historical Society: 12 and 39, 21; North Wind Picture Archives: 25 (North Wind); Courtesy of the Pierce Brigade, Concord, NH: 37 (David M. Budd Photography); Courtesy of the Redwood Library and Athenaeum, Newport, Rhode Island: 6; U.S. Air Force photo: 45.

Library of Congress Cataloging–in–Publication Data
Ferry, Steven, 1953–
  Franklin Pierce / by Steven Ferry.
    p. cm. — (Presidents of the U.S.A)
  Includes bibliographical references and index.
  ISBN 978–1–60253–043–0 (library bound : alk. paper)
  1. Pierce, Franklin, 1804–1869—Juvenile literature. 2. Presidents—United States—Biography—Juvenile literature. I. Title. II. Series.

E432.F46 2008
973.6'6092—dc22
  [B]
                                    2007049064

Franklin Pierce served as president from 1853 to 1857.

TABLE OF CONTENTS

C H A P T E R O N E

A PROMISING START

Franklin Pierce, the 14th U.S. president, was called "Young Hickory of the Granite Hills." He earned this nickname because he was born in the Granite Hills of New Hampshire and because, at the time, he was the youngest man ever elected president. Franklin Pierce lived during a time of tremendous change. Some of the problems that he had to deal with Americans are still struggling with today. These include how people of different races and cultures treat each other; the dangers of drinking alcohol; and the costs of war in terms of both lives lost and money spent.

Franklin Pierce in 1853

Franklin Pierce was born in Hillsborough, New Hampshire. His father, Benjamin, was one of the town's earliest settlers. As a young man, Benjamin had joined the army to help the American colonies win their independence from Great Britain. After nine years of war, Benjamin returned to Hillsborough as

The Pierce family
home in Hillsborough,
New Hampshire.
To date, Pierce is
the only president to
have been born in
New Hampshire.

a hero. He soon married Anna Kendrick. Over their years together, Benjamin and Anna had eight children. Franklin, who was born on November 23, 1804, was their seventh child.

Like his brothers and sisters before him, Franklin was born in a small log cabin. Soon after his birth, the family moved to a spacious house that Benjamin Pierce had built for them. As a young boy, Franklin listened to exciting stories about the War of 1812. Two of his

Benjamin Pierce served in the Continental army throughout the American Revolution. He fought in the Battle of Bunker Hill and survived the freezing winter at Valley Forge.

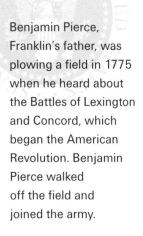

Benjamin Pierce, Franklin's father, was plowing a field in 1775 when he heard about the Battles of Lexington and Concord, which began the American Revolution. Benjamin Pierce walked off the field and joined the army.

older brothers had joined the army, just as their father had years before. Franklin hoped to one day serve his country. He often listened to his father give speeches in support of President James Madison and the war.

Benjamin Pierce had not had the advantage of a good education, but he insisted his sons should have the best schooling possible. Franklin began attending school as a young boy, and he soon learned to read. He was a fast learner and often helped tutor other students during recess. By age 16, he was ready for college and enrolled at Bowdoin (pronounced BOW-dun) College in Brunswick, Maine.

At first, Franklin's grades at Bowdoin were not very good. He often skipped classes to spend time with his friends. Luckily, two classmates convinced him to try harder. For three months, Franklin woke up at four o'clock each morning and studied until midnight. He became such a good student that he taught classes at a small schoolhouse during his vacation.

Bowdoin College was founded in 1794. Franklin Pierce attended the school in the 1820s, at the same time as the writers Nathaniel Hawthorne and Henry Wadsworth Longfellow.

By the time Pierce graduated from Bowdoin in 1824, he was one of the school's best students, graduating third in his class. An excellent public speaker, Franklin decided to study law. In September 1827, he passed his law exams and became a lawyer. That same year, his father was elected governor of New Hampshire. Pierce decided to follow in his father's footsteps and enter **politics.** In 1829, Franklin Pierce was elected to political office for the first time. He was just 24 years old when he became a **representative** to the New Hampshire legislature.

Both Franklin Pierce and his father were members of the Democratic Party. This **political party** was founded by President Andrew Jackson and his friends. The Democrats promised to protect the rights of ordinary Americans. They also wanted to keep the **federal** government from gaining too much power. The Democrats believed the states should be able to make laws for themselves. Both Franklin Pierce and his father were happy when Andrew Jackson (known as "Old Hickory") was elected president in 1828.

Nathaniel Hawthorne wrote a biography of Pierce that Pierce used during his presidential campaign of 1852.

Andrew Jackson became a national hero during the War of 1812. He was nicknamed "Old Hickory" because he was famously tough, like the wood of the hickory tree.

Pierce remained in the state legislature for four years. He served as the speaker of the house, the leader who takes charge of the meetings. He was also the head of the education committee. In 1832, New Hampshire voters elected Pierce, who was not yet 30 years old, to the U.S. House of Representatives. He moved to Washington, D.C., where he served as a representative for four years.

Pierce was the first president born in the 19th century.

The cabin in which Franklin Pierce was born is now under water. A river was dammed to create a lake, which is called Franklin Pierce Lake.

Franklin Pierce married Jane Appleton in 1834. The two had little in common. He was outgoing; she was shy. He supported President Andrew Jackson; her family detested Jackson.

Soon after moving to Washington, Pierce married Jane Means Appleton. Jane was a quiet, shy, very religious woman. Pierce was fun loving and outgoing. He loved to attend parties and meet new people. Jane disapproved of drinking alcohol, but her husband enjoyed meetings his friends at a local tavern for drinks and conversation. This made life difficult for Jane. She did not like to see her husband drinking.

At this time, many people felt drinking alcohol was dangerous. Some people became involved in the **temperance movement.** The aim of this movement was to get people to drink less or, in some cases, to ban the sale of alcohol entirely. Jane Pierce was involved in the temperance movement.

Franklin's personality made him popular in Washington, and he was a success in politics. Jane hated politics and life in the capital. She often tried to convince Franklin to leave Washington. He always refused, and the couple often quarreled. Still, Franklin tried to be kind and loving to his wife. Finally, Jane returned to New Hampshire. In 1836, she had their first child, Franklin Jr., but the baby died when he was just three days old. It was the first of many personal tragedies that would haunt the Pierces throughout their lives together.

Franklin Pierce was elected to the New Hampshire legislature in 1829, the same year his father began his second term as governor.

One story says that Franklin and Jane Pierce met at Bowdoin College during a thunderstorm. Jane was running across campus when it started to rain. She dashed under a tree for shelter, and Franklin ran to rescue her. He picked her up in his arms and took her to safety.

THE COST OF LIVING

In 1829, Pierce moved to Concord, New Hampshire, to serve in the state legislature. At first, he stayed at a boardinghouse, paying the owner 50¢ a day. Many out-of-town legislators stayed in boardinghouses. It was much cheaper than taking a room at the Eagle Coffee House (above), a local inn that cost $1 a day. But the Eagle was closer to the statehouse, and many legislators would have preferred to stay there.

When Pierce became the speaker of the house, he received a raise in pay. The legislature now paid him $2.50 a day. He could afford to stay at the Eagle Coffee House. How did he spend the rest of his money during his first term? He bought seven bottles of wine for $1 each and many 3¢ cigars. He spent 50¢ when he needed to get his "boots blacked" (his shoes shined). It cost $3.40 to board his horse for 17 nights and another $4.90 for the three bushels of oats the horse ate.

CHAPTER TWO

LIFE IN POLITICS

For many years, problems had been growing between the northern and southern states. Many northerners wanted to do away with slavery. Southerners depended on slave labor to run large farms called plantations. While Pierce was in Congress, the situation grew worse. Although he was from the North, Pierce did not believe slavery should be **abolished,** or outlawed. Instead, Pierce thought the states should decide for themselves whether to allow slavery.

Pierce thought the best way for the **Union** to stay together was for the North and the South to **compromise.** This meant that both sides would have to give up part of what they wanted in order to reach an agreement. Throughout Pierce's career, slavery would be the most pressing issue facing the nation.

Pierce was elected to the U.S. Senate in 1836. He usually voted with the Democratic Party. He voted against the party only one time. Some Democrats wanted to make a rule that would stop senators from suggesting new laws about slavery. Pierce was against this. He felt that people who were against slavery, who were called **abolitionists,** should be able to express

A fight breaks out at an abolitionist meeting in Boston. Pierce believed that abolitionists must be allowed to explain their views, in Congress and elsewhere.

their views. Pierce felt if the abolitionists were not allowed to speak in the Senate, more problems between the North and the South would arise. Other than this, Pierce was always loyal to his party.

The Pierces' second son, Frank Robert, was born in 1839. Jane Pierce lived with the baby in New Hampshire, while Franklin stayed in Washington, D.C. Jane wanted her husband to return to his family, especially after their third son, Benjamin, was born. Pierce gave up his Senate seat in 1842 and began practicing law in Concord, New Hampshire. This made his wife happy, but her happiness was short-lived. Frank Robert died in 1843, when he was just four years old. It was another sad time for the Pierces.

Pierce did not want to leave politics completely. But he took part only in local politics so that he would be close to Jane and Benjamin. Pierce managed James Polk's presidential campaign in New Hampshire. After he was elected president, Polk did not forget Pierce's work. In 1845, he named Pierce the district attorney

Pierce worked to get Democrat James K. Polk elected president in 1844. Polk admired Pierce's political skills and offered him several jobs.

Franklin Pierce joined the military in 1846. Although he lacked military experience, he led troops in the Mexican-American War in 1847.

for New Hampshire. This meant Pierce was in charge of the state's legal matters. The following year, the president asked Pierce to join his cabinet, his group of closest advisers. Taking the job would have meant returning to Washington, D.C., and Pierce knew Jane would never agree to it.

Pierce wrote to Polk, turning down the offer. "Although the early years of my manhood were devoted to public life," he wrote, "it was never really suited to my taste. I longed . . . for the quiet and independence that belong only to the private citizen." Pierce said that when he retired from the Senate he had promised never to leave his family again. He told President Polk that nothing could change his mind—unless the nation went to war.

And that is exactly what happened. In 1846, like his father and brothers before him, Pierce joined the army to fight for his country. The United States was at war with Mexico, battling for control of Texas. Pierce entered the army as a private, the lowest rank of soldier. He asked Polk to make him an officer. Pierce was granted the title of brigadier general and put in charge of 2,500 soldiers.

During Pierce's time, the Democratic Party was also called the Jacksonian Party.

Pierce had no experience in the military, and he was not a great soldier. In one battle, he was knocked unconscious when he was thrown from his horse. In another battle, he twisted his knee and fainted. Because of his frequent accidents, some soldiers referred to him as "Fainting Frank." In July 1847, Pierce led his troops on a march to Mexico City. Despite his stomach problems and saddle blisters, he stayed with the army until it captured Mexico City in September.

Pierce liked to fish during his spare time.

Pierce did not like to speak on the floor of Congress; he preferred to work on committees.

Pierce resigned from the army in 1848 and returned home. New Hampshire residents welcomed him as a hero, but Pierce was disappointed. He had hoped to gain glory as a soldier. He felt he had let down himself and his country. He returned to practicing law and lived quietly in Concord with his wife and son.

Pierce's vice presidential running mate was William King of Alabama. King was ill throughout the campaign and died a month after being sworn in as vice president. No one was named to replace him.

A popular slogan during the time of Pierce's presidential campaign was "We Polked you in 1844; we shall Pierce you in 1852!"

Pierce supported laws to end slavery in Washington, D.C., and to let California become a state.

Perhaps life would have been good to the Pierce family if Franklin had kept his promise to stay out of national politics. But he did not. The Democrats were unable to agree on a presidential **candidate** in 1852. After 34 **ballots,** no one had won the **nomination.** Finally, some of Pierce's friends suggested he would be a good candidate. Jane Pierce was so upset when she heard the news that she fainted.

It took 15 more ballots before the Democrats nominated Pierce. The Democrats did not choose him because they believed he would be a good leader—they simply couldn't agree on anyone else! Southerners voted for Pierce because he approved of slavery in the South. Many of Pierce's friends were southerners. Northerners voted for him because he had done so little in politics that he hadn't made any enemies. Pierce's vice presidential running mate was a southerner, Senator William R. King of Alabama.

Pierce's opponent in the presidential election was his former commander during the Mexican-American War, General Winfield Scott. Scott and his supporters said many nasty things about Pierce during the campaign. Scott said that Pierce had acted like a coward during the war. The Democrats fought back by telling people that Pierce had always been a strong supporter of President Andrew Jackson, who was quite popular. They called Pierce "Young Hickory," reminding voters of Andrew Jackson's nickname, "Old Hickory."

General Winfield Scott published a tiny book about Pierce during the presidential campaign. Scott had a very low opinion of Pierce. Scott's book claimed to list all of Pierce's heroic deeds during the Mexican-American War. The pages were blank!

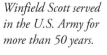

Winfield Scott served in the U.S. Army for more than 50 years.

Jane Pierce and her son, Benjamin. At age 11, Benjamin died in a train accident.

In some ways, Pierce was a natural politician. He liked to meet and talk with people. He was good at remembering names and faces. He promised favors to people if they elected him. After a close election, Pierce became the new president.

Unfortunately, things went wrong before he even took office. In January 1853, the Pierces were traveling by train when tragedy struck again. Their train went off the tracks. Franklin and Jane Pierce received only minor injuries in the accident. But young Benjamin, the Pierces' only living son, was killed before his parents' eyes.

SHADOW OF THE WHITE HOUSE

Jane Pierce never wanted her husband to be president. She hated politics and wanted to lead a quiet life. Jane was a serious woman. She felt being a politician's wife demanded a cheerful personality and a love of parties, neither of which she had.

After the Pierces' first two sons died, Jane focused all her attention on her sole surviving child, Benjamin. The Pierces called him Bennie. After Bennie died in a train accident in January 1853, Jane refused to travel to Washington. She did not think she could bear life in the nation's capital. In fact, she felt certain God had taken Bennie so her husband would have fewer things on his mind when he became president. Pierce entered the presidency alone and under a cloud of great sorrow. His wife's behavior upset him even more. He began to think of Bennie's death as punishment for his faults.

Jane Pierce eventually joined her husband in Washington. For the first two years of his presidency, Jane rarely left her living quarters at the White House. She went out only to attend church. She left the hostess duties of the first lady to a friend, preferring to pray and write sad letters to her dead son. People began to call her "the Shadow of the White House."

Finally, in 1855, Jane began to appear at her husband's side when guests visited the White House. Although she always greeted people with a smile, visitors said that her face still bore the signs of grief. One guest recalled his visit to the White House with these words, "Everything in that mansion seems cold and cheerless. I have seen hundreds of log cabins which seemed to contain more happiness."

CHAPTER THREE

AN UNHAPPY PRESIDENT

So began Pierce's presidency. Both he and his wife were upset by the recent loss of their son. Jane was too sad to go with her husband to Washington. Pierce's **inauguration** took place on a gray and snowy day that was like the president's mood. He could scarcely face the huge responsibility of the presidency after this tragedy.

"You have summoned me in my weakness," Pierce said in his inaugural address on March 4, 1853. He asked Americans to support him with their strength. He also stated how well the United States was doing and how it should continue to grow peacefully. He promised to protect the rights of the states that were guaranteed by the **Constitution**—including slavery. He said that the issue of slavery would not destroy the Union.

Franklin Pierce, nicknamed "Handsome Frank," became president in 1853.

Pierce had some success as president. He signed a **treaty** that allowed American fishermen to fish in the waters off Canada. In return, the Canadians could sell their products in the United States without paying taxes.

Another important achievement during Pierce's presidency had been begun by Millard Fillmore, the prior president. The Japanese had long refused to allow Americans and Europeans into their country. President Fillmore wanted to open trade with Japan, so he sent U.S. Navy commodore Matthew Perry there with four ships. Perry arrived in Tokyo Bay in July 1853, shortly after Pierce became president. Commodore Perry gave the Japanese a letter from Fillmore requesting that the Japanese consider trading with the United States. In March 1854, Perry and the Japanese signed a treaty of peace and friendship that opened trade between the two countries.

Supporters wave their hats in the air while Pierce gives his inauguration speech. Pierce was an accomplished speaker. He was the first president to give his inauguration speech from memory rather than by reading notes.

Franklin Pierce is the only president who said, "I promise" instead of "I swear" at the ceremony when he took office.

IMMIGRANTS VS. "KNOW-NOTHINGS"

The United States has always opened its doors to people from other countries. Sometimes tensions arise between new immigrants and people who have been in the country for longer.

Between 1830 and 1860, about five million immigrants arrived in the United States. In Pierce's time, most new immigrants lived in the cities of Boston, New York, and Chicago. The image above shows immigrants getting off a boat in New York City. The immigrants had to accept jobs for low pay. They took hard, dirty jobs in construction and trades, jobs that no one else wanted. Immigrants sometimes competed for jobs against African Americans who lived in northern cities.

Many of the immigrants in this period were Irish Catholics. In the 1850s, the Know-Nothing Party was formed to oppose the new immigrants. They feared that Catholics were more devoted to their church than to the country. They wanted immigrants to have to wait 21 years before they would be able to become citizens and vote. They also believed that only Protestants should be allowed to be public school teachers.

In 1854, the Know-Nothings won many state and local elections across the country. But the Know-Nothings were divided over the issue of slavery. As slavery became the dominant issue of the day, the Know-Nothings faded away.

When the United States won its war with Mexico, it had taken control of a huge amount of land including what are now the states of California, Nevada, and Utah, and parts of New Mexico, Arizona, Colorado, and Wyoming. By the time Pierce became president, there was still no railroad line to the West Coast.

The United States was eager to build one. As it stood, most passengers and trade goods from the Atlantic Coast had to travel by ship around the tip of South America. The voyage took several months. Once the railroad was built, the cross-country trip could be made in less than a week. People believed that one of the best railroad routes to California would pass through the hot desert land in what is now southern Arizona. But in early 1853, that land still belonged to Mexico.

Pierce set about expanding the Union, as he had promised to do at his inauguration. He ordered the purchase of nearly 30,000 square miles of land from Mexico for $10 million. It was named the Gadsden Purchase,

Pierce is the only president who kept all the members of his cabinet throughout his term.

Pierce was the first president to have central heating in the White House.

In 1854, the United States made the Gadsden Purchase. The land included in the purchase is now part of Arizona and New Mexico.

after James Gadsden, the American official who worked out the deal. With this new land, which was added to Arizona and New Mexico, the United States could build a southern railroad to the Pacific Ocean.

After the Gadsden Purchase, Pierce wanted to increase the size of the nation even more. He tried to convince the British to give the United States part of the coast of Central America. Adventurers called **filibusters** traveled to Nicaragua to support Pierce's idea. Many northerners disapproved of this idea because slavery would be legal in the region. They believed Pierce was trying to increase not only the size of the nation but also the number of slave states.

Southerners and northerners had the same disagreements over Cuba. Southerners wanted this island,

William Walker led a group of filibusters to Nicaragua in 1855. He seized power and named himself president. In 1857, Nicaraguans battled Walker's forces (below), and Walker was forced to leave the country.

which lies about 90 miles off the tip of Florida, to become part of the United States. They believed its sugar plantations and slave trade could help slavery survive and expand. Pierce and his many southern advisers decided to offer Spain $130 million for Cuba. They threatened that if Spain did not accept the offer, the United States would take Cuba by force.

When northerners learned of the plan, they were furious. They claimed the plan to take over Cuba was just another way to strengthen slavery. Pierce and his advisers had to give up on the idea.

The battle over slavery soon grew even more fierce. In May 1854, Congress passed the Kansas-Nebraska Act. Kansas and Nebraska had been free **territories** since the Missouri Compromise of 1820, which had

While in office, Pierce was arrested for running over an old woman with his horse, but the case was dismissed due to a lack of evidence.

FREE STATE
CONVENTION!

All persons who are favorable to a union of effort, and a permanent organization of all the Free State elements of Kansas Territory, and who wish to secure upon the broadest platform the co-operation of all who agree upon this point, are requested to meet at their several places of holding elections, in their respective districts on the 25th of August, instant, at one o'clock, P. M., and appoint five delegates to each representative to which they were entitled in the Legislative Assembly, who shall meet in general Convention at

Big Springs, Wednesday, Sept. 5th '55,

at 10 o'clock A. M., for the purpose of adopting a Platform upon which all may act harmoniously who prefer Freedom to Slavery.

The nomination of a Delegate to Congress, will also come up before the General Convention.

Let no sectional or party issues distract or prevent the perfect co-operation of Free State men. Union and harmony are absolutely necessary to success. The pro-slavery party are fully and effectually organized. No jars nor minor issues divide them. And to contend against them successfully, we also must be united.— Without prudence and harmony of action we are certain to fail. Let every man then do his duty and we are certain of victory.

All Free State men, without distinction, are earnestly requested to take immediate and effective steps to insure a full and correct representation for every District in the Territory. "United we stand; divided we fall."

By order of the Executive Committee of the Free State Party of the Territory of Kansas, as per resolution of the Mass Convention in session at Lawrence, Aug 15th and 16th, 1855.

J. K. GOODIN, Sec'y.

C. ROBINSON, Chairman.

Herald of Freedom, Print.

A poster announces a convention for people who wanted Kansas to be a Free State, that is, to outlaw slavery. At another convention in Kansas later in 1855, Free Staters wrote a state constitution banning slavery.

made slavery illegal in regions north of Missouri. But the new act allowed settlers in Kansas and Nebraska to decide for themselves whether to allow slavery.

With the new law, arguments over slavery grew louder. Many abolitionists went to live in Kansas. They believed that if more people who opposed slavery lived there, they would have a better chance of turning the territory against it. People who were in favor of slavery did the same thing.

Fighting soon broke out in Kansas. The situation grew worse when supporters of slavery won the vote to make Kansas a slave territory. Slavery supporters had cast 6,300 votes, but only about 1,500 people who supported slavery actually lived in the area. About

4,000 pro-slavery voters had traveled to Kansas from Missouri to cast illegal votes.

Most members of the Kansas legislature were in favor of slavery. They refused to allow a new vote. To fight back, abolitionists set up their own government. Pierce did not take time to hear both sides of the story. Instead, he said the abolitionist government was a form of **rebellion.** He ordered it to disband and sent in troops to enforce his decision.

Pierce's actions did not help calm the situation. In fact, problems grew worse because the abolitionists did not give up. In the spring of 1856, a **civil war** broke out in the territory. Pro-slavery forces broke into the homes of abolitionists and burned down buildings.

Thousands of pro-slavery Missourians crossed the border into Kansas to vote in the territorial election in 1855. Because of their votes, the territorial legislature was filled with people who favored slavery.

Abolitionist John Brown decided to fight back by organizing an attack on his pro-slavery neighbors. Brown and six other men, including four of his sons, broke into several cabins and murdered five men. Soon, warfare was raging throughout the territory. By the time peace returned, more than two hundred people had been killed. Americans called the territory "Bleeding Kansas."

John Brown (kissing baby) left Kansas soon after his attack on pro-slavery settlers. In 1859, he tried to steal weapons from a site in what is now West Virginia. He planned to arm slaves for an uprising. Brown was soon captured, however. In this picture, Brown is on his way to be hanged.

BROOKS ATTACKS SUMNER

The violence of 1856 was not limited to Kansas.
Battles even took place on the floor of Congress. In
May, Senator Charles Sumner of Massachusetts gave a
bitter, dramatic speech against people who supported
slavery. He even insulted some of his fellow senators. The
speech was later called "the Crime Against Kansas."

When Representative Preston Brooks of South
Carolina heard about the speech, he was furious. He
rushed onto the Senate floor and found Sumner seated
at his desk. Brooks beat Sumner brutally with his walking
stick until Sumner collapsed to the floor, bleeding.

Some members of Congress tried to get Brooks
removed from the House. But many people from the South
were proud of what Brooks had done. In fact, Brooks
won the next election by unanimous vote, meaning he
received every vote cast. It took Sumner more than three
years to heal from his injuries, and northerners left his
seat empty as a symbol of the attack upon him.

A SAD ENDING

After the problems in Kansas, the Democrats lost faith in Franklin Pierce. Still, near the end of his term, Pierce felt he could claim "a peaceful condition of things in Kansas." He hoped the Democrats would choose him as their candidate in the next election. But his party did not think he could win. The fighting in Kansas had been too damaging. They also felt that in such a troubled time, Pierce could not provide the leadership the nation needed. The Democrats instead chose James Buchanan as their candidate. To the relief of Jane Pierce, she and Franklin would soon leave the White House.

Franklin Pierce in 1858

After President James Buchanan took office, the Pierces began a long tour of Europe, the West Indies, and the United States. Jane Pierce's health had grown worse during her husband's presidency. Franklin Pierce hoped the travel would improve her health and cheer her up. She

was still grieving the loss of her children. She carried Bennie's Bible with her wherever she went. Finally, in 1860, the couple returned to Concord to be near family and friends. They had been away for three years.

By this time, the disagreements over slavery between the North and the South were bringing the country to the brink of civil war. "I wish I [had] higher hope for the future of our country," said Pierce after he arrived home. "But the aspect of any vision is fearfully dark."

President Pierce at a White House reception. Pierce wanted to run for a second term, but many Americans felt he had not been an effective president. In 1856, the Democrats instead nominated James Buchanan as their presidential candidate.

Northern and Southern troops battle in western Virginia in 1862.

Like Pierce, President Buchanan had not been able to solve the conflict during his four years in office. In fact, many Americans felt that he, too, had made the situation worse.

That November, Abraham Lincoln was elected president. Unlike Pierce and Buchanan, Lincoln was a member of the Republican Party, which opposed the spread of slavery. More than anything, Lincoln wanted to hold the United States together at any cost. But Southern states were convinced that Lincoln would immediately outlaw slavery once he entered office. Soon after he was elected, they began to **secede** from the Union. By April 1861, the nation was at war with itself.

When the Civil War began, Pierce was a bitter enemy of President Lincoln. He criticized the Union for its actions during the war. He wrote to an old friend, saying, "If I were in the Southerners' places, after so many years of aggression, I should probably be doing what they are doing." Such talk made Pierce unpopular in New Hampshire. He lost many of his friends and supporters, who believed he was a **traitor.**

To add to his sorrow, Jane died in 1863. Although their marriage had sometimes been difficult, he had always loved her very much and tried to do as she wished. Jane Pierce was buried near her children's graves at the Old North Cemetery in Concord.

After Abraham Lincoln was **assassinated,** a mob threatened to attack Franklin Pierce's home. They were angry that he had criticized Lincoln.

Abraham Lincoln served as president throughout the Civil War. He was assassinated just days after the South surrendered.

Pierce spent his last years alone. He had not touched a drop of alcohol for more than 20 years, in part to please Jane. But he began to drink heavily after her death. His health began to fail during the summer of 1869. He died on October 8 and was buried next to his wife and children.

Franklin Pierce has not gone down in history as a good president. He entered the presidency during one of the most difficult periods in U.S. history, when Americans had to decide the future of slavery. He was not able to solve the problem, and the situation grew worse while he was president. But Pierce was an honest man who wanted to uphold the Constitution. His old friend Nathaniel Hawthorne once wrote that Pierce "has in him many of the chief elements of a great ruler." Unfortunately, President Pierce was not able to live up to such great hopes.

Pierce's home in Concord, New Hampshire is now open to visitors. The house has been restored to look much like it did in Pierce's time. Many pieces of furniture in the house once belonged to Pierce.

THE FAITH OF FRANKLIN PIERCE

Pierce was raised an Episcopalian but was a bit lazy about practicing his faith as a young man. In his last year at Bowdoin College, this changed. He prayed every night with a friend. When he married Jane, she insisted that they read the Bible and say their prayers each day. But while he lived away from home, Pierce did not practice his religion so faithfully.

Later, when their third son died, Pierce began to think his children had been taken from him as punishment for ignoring religion. "We should have lived for God," he wrote in his diary, "and have left the dear ones to the care of Him who is alone able to take care of them and us." Pierce began to attend church regularly. As president, he read prayers each day, said grace at each meal, and was so strict about not working on Sunday that he even refused to read his mail. Many members of the White House staff went to church out of respect for the president and first lady.

Pierce drifted away from the church after his wife's death in 1863. But after a severe illness the next year, he became active in his church once more. When he died in 1869, Pierce had made his peace with God. He believed that after death, he would go on to a better life. Pierce is buried at the Old North Cemetery in Concord.

1800

1804
Franklin Pierce is born in Hillsborough, New Hampshire, on November 23.

1820

1824
Pierce graduates from Bowdoin College, in Brunswick, Maine.

1827
Pierce begins to practice law in New Hampshire.

1829
New Hampshire elects Pierce to the state legislature. He holds the post until 1833.

1830

1831
Pierce is elected speaker of the house of the New Hampshire legislature. He is the youngest man ever to serve in this post.

1832
Pierce is elected to the U.S. House of Representatives. He holds the post for four years.

1834
Pierce marries Jane Means Appleton on November 10.

1836
Franklin Jr., the Pierces' first son, is born. He dies three days later. New Hampshire elects Pierce U.S. senator. He holds the position until 1842.

1839
The Pierces' second son, Frank Robert, is born.

1840

1841
The Pierces' third son, Benjamin (Bennie), is born.

1842
Pierce leaves the U.S. Senate.

1843
Frank Robert Pierce dies.

1845
President James K. Polk names Pierce the district attorney of New Hampshire.

1846
Pierce joins the army. He fights in the Mexican-American War as a brigadier general.

1848
Pierce leaves the army and returns to New Hampshire, disappointed that he had not proved to be a better soldier.

1852
Pierce is nominated as the Democratic candidate for president. He is elected in November.

1853
Benjamin Pierce is killed in a train accident. Pierce is inaugurated as president on March 4. Commodore Matthew Perry arrives in Japan, hoping to convince its leaders to begin trading with the United States. The Gadsden Purchase, in which the United States gains land in Arizona and New Mexico, is completed on December 30.

1854
Commodore Matthew Perry and Japanese leaders sign a treaty to begin trade between the United States and Japan. Congress passes the Kansas-Nebraska Act, which says that people in those territories can decide whether to allow slavery. This angers many abolitionists, because the two territories were made free by the Missouri Compromise of 1820.

1856
Fighting breaks out in Kansas between abolitionists and supporters of slavery. John Brown and his followers attack and kill five pro-slavery men. People begin calling the territory "Bleeding Kansas." The Democrats do not choose Pierce as their candidate for the next election. James Buchanan is elected the 15th president.

1857
Franklin Pierce leaves the presidency. He and Jane tour Europe, the West Indies, and the United States hoping to improve her health.

1860
Abraham Lincoln is elected president. Southern states begin to secede from the Union, fearing that he will abolish slavery.

1861
The first shots are fired between the North and the South at Fort Sumter in South Carolina on April 12. Pierce blames President Lincoln and the Union for the war.

1863
Jane Pierce dies on December 2.

1865
The Civil War ends. Abraham Lincoln is shot on April 14. He dies the next day.

1869
Franklin Pierce dies on October 8 in Concord, New Hampshire. He is buried with his wife and family at the Old North Cemetery in Concord.

GLOSSARY

abolished (uh-BAWL-isht) If something is abolished, it is ended or made illegal. Pierce did not believe that slavery should be abolished.

abolitionists (ab-uh-LISH-uh-nists) Abolitionists were people who wanted to end slavery before and during the Civil War. Pierce believed that both abolitionists and those in favor of slavery should be able to express their views.

assassinated (uh-SA-si-nayt-ed) If someone is assassinated, he or she is murdered. Abraham Lincoln was assassinated in 1865.

ballots (BA-luts) A ballot is a round of voting. It took 49 ballots for Democrats to choose Pierce as their presidential candidate in 1852.

campaign (kam-PAYN) A campaign is the process of running for an election, including activities such as giving speeches or attending rallies. Winfield Scott and his supporters said nasty things about Pierce during the presidential campaign of 1852.

candidate (KAN-duh-det) A candidate is a person running in an election. The Democrats could not agree on a presidential candidate in 1852.

civil war (SIV-il WAR) A civil war is a war between opposing groups of citizens from the same country or territory. A civil war broke out in Kansas between slaveholders and abolitionists.

compromise (KOM-pruh-myz) A compromise is a way to settle a disagreement in which both sides give up part of what they want. Pierce thought the North and the South should compromise to preserve the Union.

constitution (kon-stih-TOO-shun) A constitution is the set of basic principles that govern a state, country, or society. Pierce promised to protect states' rights that were guaranteed by the U.S. Constitution.

federal (FED-ur-ul) Federal means having to do with the central government of the United States, rather than a state or city government. The Democrats did not think the federal government should be too powerful.

filibusters (FIL-ih-bus-terz) Filibusters were American adventurers who tried to conquer Central America. During Pierce's presidency, filibusters traveled to Nicaragua.

immigrants (IM-uh-grents) Immigrants are people who move to a new country to live. Between 1830 and 1860, about five million immigrants moved to the United States.

inauguration (ih-nawg-yuh-RAY-shun) An inauguration is the ceremony that takes place when a new president begins a term. Pierce's inauguration took place on a gray, snowy day.

nomination (nom-ih-NAY-shun) If someone receives a nomination, he or she is chosen by a political party to run for an office. Pierce won the Democratic presidential nomination in 1852.

political party (puh-LIT-ih-kul PAR-tee) A political party is a group of people who share similar ideas about how to run a government. The Democratic Party is a political party.

politics (PAHL-ih-tiks) Politics refers to the actions and practices of the government. Like his father, Pierce was interested in politics.

rebellion (ri-BEL-yun) A rebellion is a fight against one's government. Pierce said the abolitionist government in Kansas was a form of rebellion.

representative (rep-ree-ZEN-tuh-tiv) A representative is someone who attends a meeting, having agreed to speak or act for others. Pierce became a representative to the New Hampshire legislature in 1829.

secede (seh-SEED) If a group secedes, it separates from a larger group. Southern states began to secede from the Union after Abraham Lincoln was elected president.

temperance movement (TEM-prunts MOOV-munt) The temperance movement was a movement that encouraged people not to drink alcohol. Jane Pierce supported the temperance movement.

territories (TAIR-uh-tor-eez) Territories are lands or regions, especially lands that belong to a government. Civil war broke out in the territory of Kansas in 1856.

traitor (TRAY-ter) A traitor is someone who betrays his or her country. People accused Pierce of being a traitor when he criticized President Lincoln.

treaty (TREE-tee) A treaty is a formal agreement between nations. Japan and the United States signed a treaty of friendship that opened trade between the two countries in 1854.

union (YOON-yen) A union is the joining together of two people or groups of people, such as states. The Union is another name for the United States.

THE UNITED STATES GOVERNMENT

The United States government is divided into three equal branches: the executive, the legislative, and the judicial. This division helps prevent abuses of power because each branch has to answer to the other two. No one branch can become too powerful.

EXECUTIVE BRANCH

PRESIDENT
VICE PRESIDENT
DEPARTMENTS

The job of the executive branch is to enforce the laws. It is headed by the president, who serves as the spokesperson for the United States around the world. The president signs bills into law and appoints important officials such as federal judges. He or she is also the commander in chief of the U.S. military. The president is assisted by the vice president, who takes over if the president dies or cannot carry out the duties of the office.

The executive branch also includes various departments, each focused on a specific topic. They include the Defense Department, the Justice Department, and the Agriculture Department. The department heads, along with other officials such as the vice president, serve as the president's closest advisers, called the cabinet.

LEGISLATIVE BRANCH

CONGRESS
*Senate and
House of Representatives*

The job of the legislative branch is to make the laws. It consists of Congress, which is divided into two parts: the Senate and the House of Representatives. The Senate has 100 members, and the House of Representatives has 435 members. Each state has two senators. The number of representatives a state has varies depending on the state's population.

Besides making laws, Congress also passes budgets and enacts taxes. In addition, it is responsible for declaring war, maintaining the military, and regulating trade with other countries.

JUDICIAL BRANCH

SUPREME COURT
COURTS OF APPEALS
DISTRICT COURTS

The job of the judicial branch is to interpret the laws. It consists of the nation's federal courts. Trials are held in district courts. During trials, judges must decide what laws mean and how they apply. Courts of appeals review the decisions made in district courts.

The nation's highest court is the Supreme Court. If someone disagrees with a court of appeals ruling, he or she can ask the Supreme Court to review it. The Supreme Court may refuse. The Supreme Court makes sure that decisions and laws do not violate the Constitution.

CHOOSING
THE PRESIDENT

I t may seem odd, but American voters don't elect the president directly. Instead, the president is chosen using what is called the Electoral College.

Each state gets as many votes in the Electoral College as its combined total of senators and representatives in Congress. For example, Iowa has two senators and five representatives, so it gets seven electoral votes. Although the District of Columbia does not have any voting members in Congress, it gets three electoral votes. Usually, the candidate who wins the most votes in any given state receives all of that state's electoral votes.

To become president, a candidate must get more than half of the Electoral College votes. There are a total of 538 votes in the Electoral College, so a candidate needs 270 votes to win. If nobody receives 270 Electoral College votes, the House of Representatives chooses the president.

With the Electoral College system, the person who receives the most votes nationwide does not always receive the most electoral votes. This happened most recently in 2000, when Al Gore received half a million more national votes than George W. Bush. Bush became president because he had more Electoral College votes.

THE WHITE HOUSE

The White House is the official home of the president of the United States. It is located at 1600 Pennsylvania Avenue NW in Washington, D.C. In 1792, a contest was held to select the architect who would design the president's home. James Hoban won. Construction took eight years.

The first president, George Washington, never lived in the White House. The second president, John Adams, moved into the house in 1800, though the inside was not yet complete. During the War of 1812, British soldiers burned down much of the White House. It was rebuilt several years later.

The White House was changed through the years. Porches were added, and President Theodore Roosevelt added the West Wing. President William Taft changed the shape of the presidential office, making it into the famous Oval Office. While Harry Truman was president, the old house was discovered to be structurally weak. All the walls were reinforced with steel, and the rooms were rebuilt.

Today, the White House has 132 rooms (including 35 bathrooms), 28 fireplaces, and 3 elevators. It takes 570 gallons of paint to cover the outside of the six-story building. The White House provides the president with many ways to relax. It includes a putting green, a jogging track, a swimming pool, a tennis court, and beautifully landscaped gardens. The White House also has a movie theater, a billiard room, and a one-lane bowling alley.

PRESIDENTIAL PERKS

The job of president of the United States is challenging. It is probably one of the most stressful jobs in the world. Because of this, presidents are paid well, though not nearly as well as the leaders of large corporations. In 2007, the president earned $400,000 a year. Presidents also receive extra benefits that make the demanding job a little more appealing.

★ **Camp David:** In the 1940s, President Franklin D. Roosevelt chose this heavily wooded spot in the mountains of Maryland to be the presidential retreat, where presidents can relax. Even though it is a retreat, world business is conducted there. Most famously, President Jimmy Carter met with Middle Eastern leaders at Camp David in 1978. The result was a peace agreement between Israel and Egypt.

★ *Air Force One*: The president flies on a jet called *Air Force One*. It is a Boeing 747-200B that has been modified to meet the president's needs.

Air Force One is the size of a large home. It is equipped with a dining room, sleeping quarters, a conference room, and office space. It also has two kitchens that can provide food for up to 50 people.

★ **The Secret Service:** While not the most glamorous of the president's perks, the Secret Service is one of the most important. The Secret Service is a group of highly trained agents who protect the president and the president's family.

★ **The Presidential State Car:** The presidential limousine is a stretch Cadillac DTS.

It has been armored to protect the president in case of attack. Inside the plush car are a foldaway desk, an entertainment center, and a communications console.

★ **The Food:** The White House has five chefs who will make any food the president wants. The White House also has an extensive wine collection.

★ **Retirement:** A former president receives a pension, or retirement pay, of just under $180,000 a year. Former presidents also receive Secret Service protection for the rest of their lives.

FACTS

QUALIFICATIONS

To run for president, a candidate must

* be at least 35 years old
* be a citizen who was born in the United States
* have lived in the United States for 14 years

TERM OF OFFICE

A president's term of office is four years.
No president can stay in office for more than two terms.

ELECTION DATE

The presidential election takes place every four years on the first Tuesday of November.

INAUGURATION DATE

Presidents are inaugurated on January 20.

OATH OF OFFICE

I do solemnly swear I will faithfully execute the office of the President of the United States and will to the best of my ability preserve, protect, and defend the Constitution of the United States.

WRITE A LETTER TO THE PRESIDENT

One of the best things about being a U.S. citizen is that Americans get to participate in their government. They can speak out if they feel government leaders aren't doing their jobs. They can also praise leaders who are going the extra mile. Do you have something you'd like the president to do? Should the president worry more about the environment and encourage people to recycle? Should the government spend more money on our schools? You can write a letter to the president to say how you feel!

1600 Pennsylvania Avenue
Washington, D.C. 20500
You can even send an e-mail to: president@whitehouse.gov

BOOKS

DiConsiglio, John D. *Franklin Pierce.* New York: Children's Press, 2004.

Feinberg, Barbara Silberdick. *America's First Ladies.* New York: Franklin Watts, 1998.

Hawthorne, Nathaniel. *The Life of Franklin Pierce.* Amsterdam, the Netherlands: Fredonia Books, 2002.

Ochoa, George. *The Fall of Mexico City.* Englewood Cliffs, NJ: Silver Burdett Press, 1989.

Somervill, Barbara A. *Franklin Pierce.* Minneapolis: Compass Point Books, 2003.

Venezia, Mike. *Franklin Pierce.* New York: Children's Press, 2005.

Young, Jeff C. *Franklin Pierce.* Berkeley Heights, NJ: MyReportLinks.com, 2002.

Zamora, Dulce. *How To Draw: The Life And Times Of Franklin Pierce (Kid's Guide to Drawing the Presidents of the United States of America).* New York: PowerKids Press, 2006.

VIDEOS

The History Channel Presents The Presidents. DVD (New York: A&E Home Video, 2005).

National Geographic's Inside the White House. DVD (Washington, DC: National Geographic Video, 2003).

INTERNET SITES

Visit our Web page for lots of links about Franklin Pierce and other U.S. presidents:

http://www.childsworld.com/links

Note to Parents, Teachers, and Librarians: We routinely verify our Web links to make sure they are safe, active sites—so encourage your readers to check them out!

INDEX